The Darling Family:
A Duet for Three

A PLAY BY
LINDA GRIFFITHS

The Darling Family

A DUET FOR THREE

Blizzard Publishing • Winnipeg

The Darling Family: A Duet for Three first published 1991 by
Blizzard Publishing Ltd.
301–89 Princess St., Winnipeg, Canada R3B 1K6
© 1991 Linda Griffiths

Cover design by Terry Gallagher
Cover photo by Michael De Sadeleer
Back cover photo by Michael De Sadeleer
Printed in Canada by Hignell Printing Ltd.

Published with the assistance of
the Canada Council and the Manitoba Arts Council.

Caution

Canadian Cataloguing in Publication Data
Griffiths, Linda, 1953–
    The darling family
    Play.
    ISBN 0-921368-17-8
I. Title.
PS8563.R536D3 1991   C812/.54   C91-097092-0
PR9199.3.G753D3 1991

The Darling Family: A Duet for Three opened at Theatre Passe Muraille's Backspace January 15, 1991, with the following cast:

SHE	Linda Griffiths
HE	Alan Williams

Dramaturgy: Alan Williams
Stage Manager: Sandra Balcovski
Lighting Design: H.Y. Fung

Preface

The Darling Family: A Duet for Three was first given a
four-week independent workshop by The Laidlaw
Foundation, under the direction of Nathan Gilbert. HE and
SHE were played by Ted Wallace and Jennifer Dale. The
piece was directed and dramaturged by Clarke Rogers. I
would like to thank the participants for their invaluable
contribution to the project. The talent brought to bear and
the wholeheartedness with which the piece was
approached were a gift made in the highest spirit of the
theatre.

Two years later, *The Darling Family* received a week-
long workshop at Theatre Passe Muraille, with the help of
Peter Hinton. I read the part of SHE, Alan Williams read
HE. A new idea of how to work on the play formed, and we
decided to treat the play as a work presented by a two-
person company, rather than as a production which would
be directed, designed and "put together" in a traditional
sense. As a result of the response of the audience at the
public reading ("You don't need anything, you could just
sit at a table and do it ..."), we decided to perform the piece
on a completely bare stage. Six months later, the piece was
previewed for ten days at the Second Stage of Prairie
Theatre Exchange in Winnipeg, with Graham Ashmore as
stage manager. This production "evolved from the inside."
As two actors, working without an outside eye, we talked,
argued and rehearsed without formal rehearsals until the

first time the play was presented to the audience. From the moment the play hit the audience, the blocking was inevitable.

There is no question in my mind that the play would never have come to fruition if not for the talents of Alan Williams. As a dramaturge and actor his contribution was essential. He never wavered in his commitment to the script or the project. As an actor, his belief in the essence of the theatre, in the power of the actor, if left to himself, to tell a story, was the true "direction" of the piece. *The Darling Family* is, finally, a play that loves actors.

Linda Griffiths
March, 1991

Characters and Setting

HE and SHE almost never fight, they are almost never mean, they are almost never snide, they try to give each other the best side, they are polite, they are well read, they know things about things, they almost never fight, they almost never love.

The play is ninety minutes without intermission, set, sound, or lighting cues.

A note on conventions used in the text: Stage directions are enclosed in square brackets. Italics without brackets indicate the spoken thoughts of the two characters. At times they speak in "duets"; the slash (/) indicates when an overlap of voices begins.

[The stage area is completely bare except for a dish containing sage and matches, and two rock crystals on the floor. The two actors enter. SHE lights the sage and smudges herself with the smoke. HE smudges himself. SHE fans the smoke towards the audience, then blots the sage.]

SHE: This one looks like a European movie, all muted colours, things that don't look like anything at first, and then it's as if the camera pulls back and the focus clears. It's hot, everything is washed out. There's a white crumbling room with bodies sleeping in dirty clothes. The place is crowded, and it stinks. I know that I'm in a ghetto of some kind, that there are hundreds of rooms like this, stacked and twisted, crushed together. Crying babies, shouts, swearing, bells tolling, cross-eyed, inbred children, no one knows what year it is. I'm twelve years old and he's been watching me for a while. I can feel his eyes on me. I even wiggle my bum a little when he's around. He brought me something special to eat once, and I ate it all alone, hiding. I'm twelve years old, when I found the blood, my mother laughed, then crossed herself. "Now you're in for it." The night he comes, I sort of expect it, but I don't know what it is. My dad's got huge arms and a bloated face, big bulging brown eyes with lots of veins, all watery, like a dog's. He just hauls himself on me, pulls my legs apart, then shoves his thing up me, like a kitchen knife like a knife so far up I didn't know it could go, so far

up I think it's going to rip me in pieces, pounding away.
When he crawls off I wipe the slob from my cunt and
I get out of there. Maybe I kill him, I don't know. I can't
remember. I end up with a gang of kids, we steal food
and sleep on the street. I get sick all the time. I don't let
anyone talk to me. I know. Inside I know. I get big, the
rest of me gets really skinny. They tell me I've got one
in me. They take their fingers and shove them through
a circle, poking and poking, then they waddle around
like me. Sometimes they shove their little boys' cocks
at me, but I grab them and squeeze till they run away,
holding their little things in their hands. Sometimes
they throw some food at me. I wake up and it's there.
One of the older girls says when it starts to hurt I have
to go to the nuns. They've got some kind of place up on
the hill for people to die in. She says to go there. One
day I start to squirm, like I ate bad chickens and have
to shit yellow for days. Cramping me up. I hate it. I get
worse. I got to shit but I can't. I have to get to those
nuns, don't want people watching me on the street. I'm
starting to grunt like a pig. Where are the fucking nuns?
People look at me, squatting down by the side of the
road, panting like a goat when it gets me bad. They
know what's going on, why else would I be holding my
belly like I want to die? If they come close I'll kill
them. Holding on, got to hold on. I can see it now, top
of the hill. What are they going to do? Make me kneel
down and pray? I can't do that, I can't, ohhhh Jesus,
that's from right underneath my twot. I gotta carry it
now, carry myself in my hands. I droop down so much,
maybe it'll just fall out on the road, I'd leave it there
and go back. It's not coming out though.

I just have to get through the archway, I'm crawling
down on my hands and knees, kind of pushing back
and forth with my twot, getting scared, digging my
nails in, trying to get up to the door. I drag myself up,

I'm banging and screaming, "Jesus Mary let me in, Virgin Mary let me in." They kind of drag me in, the room's got beds and flies, old people lying still like dead people, kids with no arms, one with a big head, they're groaning and moaning, it smells of hot blood. I'm crazy now, louder than any of them, the nuns have thin lips and sour faces, "Don't touch me, don't go in there." They're putting their hands up there, I'm screaming, "No, don't do that, you'll hurt it, you'll hurt the baby." I hate my belly, I hate the baby, don't care if they hurt the baby. I'm hanging onto something, somebody's arms, I could feel her come near, she's different, she's got the voice of an angel, she's saying something I'm pulling at her so hard, ohhhhh God this is my fault I'm being punished I looked at him when my tits were growing I wiggled my ass in his face she's saying something I'm drowning she's saying, "Think of the baby, can you hear me? Think of the baby." Her voice is so sweet I can hardly I talk I say, "I don't want it, I hate it." All she says is, "The next time when it comes, think of the baby." The next time it comes, I'm begging them to kill me, take the knife, I can see the knife and put it up the same place and kill me. Don't look at me, don't look at me. The angel is slapping my face saying, "Don't go away, keep alive keep alive think of the baby." I'm so tired, they stick their arms up, I'm wild thrashing on the bed. No, no more no more not again. They say, "Bear down, bear down." I do something, they all say, "Yes it's coming." I think of the baby, they say, "Bear down again again again." I'm gone I'm gone there's nothing but I push them away and fall on the floor. I'm on my hands and knees howling and shitting there's nothing left somebody's holding my head, I heave and heave and heave. There's red and black. Then nothing. I open my eyes against the black, see a bloody bundle being carried out. I try to talk, try to say, "Show it to me, show me the baby."

But I know it's dead. I don't know if I hear it, but I hear "strangled." It's my fault. I wanted it to be dead and now it's dead.

Then all I know is craziness. Dirt and hate and craziness. Wandering the streets screaming at people in their houses. Cursing them till it's over.

***

SHE: Hello? Yes it is. It was positive?... Yes, I can. Three thirty today is fine. Thankyou ... holy shit.

***

HE: Hi.

SHE: Hi.

HE: Come on in. Do you want wine, or beer, or brandy, or ...

SHE: I'll take wine.

HE: I was just practising my guitar.

SHE: It's not loud enough.

HE: I've got to have some thought for the neighbours, although I think it all evens out in the end.

SHE: Probably does.

HE: Let's sit outside.

SHE: Okay.... Nice sky.

HE: Yeah.

SHE: I got home today and there were six guys with jackhammers tearing down my front steps, then this huge cement truck arrives and looks like it's going to pave both front yards. Then the city comes and digs this giant hole in the sidewalk. They're building a Portuguese Parthenon next door and they have to tear down my steps to do it.

HE: That's a drag.

SHE: I can hardly get into the house. There's just the edges of the steps left, like ruins.

HE: Do you have to pay for new steps?

SHE: No, they couldn't carve the steps in half to leave new steps so they had to replace mine anyway.

HE: That's one good thing.

SHE: Yeah.

HE: ... so I've been on tenterhooks all day. What did you want to talk to me about?

SHE: Oh, I don't know.

HE: I think you do.

SHE: I just ... maybe you should have a drink first.

HE: I don't want a drink. Is it that bad?

SHE: Hard to say.

HE: What is it then?

SHE: ...

HE: You're pregnant.

SHE: Yeah mon, I am.

HE: You're kidding. How do you feel?

SHE: I feel like ... I don't know ... I'm just out there, really out there.

HE: It's never happened to me.

SHE: Me either. First time.

HE: It's funny, after a while you get to think you're infertile or something.

SHE: Yeah, I thought I might be.

HE: Guess not.

SHE: Guess not.

HE: Maybe I will have a drink.... What do you want to do, do you want to talk about it?

SHE: I don't know. I guess not. I feel like I'm swimming, just swimming out there in the mid-Atlantic.

HE: Do you want to keep swimming for a while, or...

SHE: When I got the call, it was going to be a joke, I thought I was starting my period this morning, and I was going to feel like an idiot, and say, "You wouldn't believe how stupid I was, I actually thought ..." Then after they told me, I just sat there for a while, and then I realized I was staring at this blue book, and when I finally focussed to see what it was, it was your copy of the *The Silent Scream*, with that picture of the foetus on the cover.

HE: That's incredible. And then this morning did you see what I pulled out of the envelope?

SHE: I couldn't believe it. The *Pro Choice News*. I thought it was a sign.

HE: Just goes to show this household doesn't avoid those issues.

SHE: I found myself imagining what you'd do. Making up a whole thing in my head about you, thinking for you.

HE: I'm supposed to want to run, isn't that the assumed male response?

SHE: Yes.

HE: It's your choice, of course, but I'm thinking that might be a little selfish to leave it all to you if you might be influenced by what I say.

SHE: It's yours too.

HE: I thought you didn't want to talk about it. If you want to talk about it, I'll talk about it.

SHE: No, you're right, I'd rather swim.

HE: How's the swimming?

SHE: Weird.

HE: Well, it's seven o'clock now, we could see a movie, or eat, or if we went really fast we could do both. What would you like to do?

SHE: I'm not very fast. I started getting this dizzy feeling, like the earth wasn't really under my feet, like everything just took a step sideways and I wasn't on it.

HE: We don't have to see a movie, I could just work here on my own or we could watch television or you could go off on your own and think or ...

SHE: No, no, I'd like to see a movie.

HE: We could see that one where the kids find the body, that looked good, it starts at seven-forty-five.

SHE: Nooo ... let's see the one about the dog.

HE: It's got subtitles.

SHE: I could take them tonight, besides it's supposed to be warm-hearted and comforting.

HE: Okay, eight-fifteen, that would give us time to eat. Do you want to eat? What have you eaten today?

SHE: Not much.

HE: Indian food?

SHE: Sure.

HE: Let's go.

> *[SHE sways. HE holds her.]*

Are you having one of these dizzy things?

SHE: Yeah.

HE: It's okay, no hurry.

SHE: I feel like I'm making it up.

HE: Making it up so that I can almost feel it too.

SHE: I'm okay now.

HE: Are you sure?

SHE: Yeah.

> *[Nearly falls again.]*

Oh, Jesus, this is for real.

***

HE: *The way she looked, the way I felt, I let her in, in that split second, / something went in. Like some kind of miracle ...*

SHE: *The way he acted, the way he looked the way his eyes shone like the warm blue sea. It went through us like a knife ...*

HE: *It's something you read about, / I thought it would never happen to me ...*

SHE: *I thought it would never happen to me. It could be done, it could actually be done /*

HE: *There's no way, I just / feel sick inside. Don't come down hard, don't push her too hard, don't be too hard ...*

SHE: *It's not so crazy really, it's possible, but is it possible / with him?*

HE: *She's going to go through it, it's in her, / inside her ...*

SHE: *He's the father now, not just some guy ...*

HE: *Can't do it, can't do it, we should have talked / right then, dangerous to wait ...*

SHE: *I feel real, finally something real in me. He took my hand to cross the street / like there were three of us crossing the street. He felt it, it was in his hand, the way he touched, that there were three of us crossing the street.*

HE: *I can't let myself feel it. Never take her hand like that again. That would be too cruel. Help her somehow. Be clear but not cruel. How / could it have happened?*

SHE: *I know why it happened ...*

HE: *There aren't three of us crossing the street. Not now. There can't be. Not three of us crossing the street.*

***

HE: Good morning.

SHE: Hi.

HE: I made an omelette but I assumed you wouldn't be eating this morning.

SHE: No.

HE: I have to go shopping, make a couple of phone calls, then tonight is that barbecue. Do you want to go?

SHE: Don't know, can't tell yet.

HE: Just let me know. Do you want some tea?

SHE: Sure.

HE: It's already made.

SHE: How long have we known each other?

HE: Three months?

SHE: More like two and a half.

HE: If you count when I went away.

SHE: If you count when you went away, then it's three months.

HE: Or two and a half.

***

HE: Hi.

SHE: Hi. Did you have a good time?

HE: It was okay. Saw a few people, yacked away.

SHE: You stayed quite late.

HE: I couldn't leave right away.

> *[HE yawns.]*

SHE: I know, I just thought.

HE: You were the one that said that I should go.

SHE: I know, I just ...

> *Imagine what you could say, you could have a ball, you really could, a kind of complete moral authority. "There I was, coughing up my insides, passing out on*

the stairs, carrying your child, and you had to have another beer."

It doesn't matter. Do you want something to drink?

HE: *I had to have that fifth beer, if I didn't have that beer, I couldn't have faced it. Standing there while they sang Happy Birthday, thinking, the worst thing I could imagine has happened.*

I'm fine for now.

SHE: I don't want to swim anymore.

HE: Whatever you say.

SHE: I'm stoned.

HE: I thought you ran out.

SHE: On hormones. I can't help thinking about it.

HE: Me too, not an hour goes by that I ...

SHE: Five minutes, with me it's every five minutes, every minute.

HE: I can understand.

SHE: What I hate is the inevitability of it.

HE: What's inevitable?

SHE: That it will be stopped. I'm trying not to speak for you. I want to, but I'm trying not to. Maybe I should speak for you. But I won't. Okay? I won't. I'm thinking all kinds of things, like what it would be like to have it on my own. But maybe I'm wrong, maybe you're not thinking like that, I just keep trying not to speak for you. I know you have a lot of plans, I know that. I just have been assuming some things.

HE: What things?

SHE: I want to talk about it.

HE: Do you want me to talk about it too? Or do you just want to talk about it?

SHE: I want you to talk about it.

[HE yawns.]

Maybe you're tired, you've had too many beer.

HE: No, I'm fine, why do you say that?

[HE yawns again.]

SHE: Woman's intuition.

HE: Alright. It's not a time when I want to consider having a family, it's a time of flux in my life. I do have a two-year plan, I don't think it's wrong to have one, and there are a lot of things I want to do, and raising a child isn't one of them. I wouldn't want you to, but if you were to go ahead, then I would want to be involved.

SHE: That's what I thought.

The iron has entered my soul.

HE: Sorry to disappoint you.

SHE: *What about the look on his face when I told him?*

HE: There's also the short time we've known each other.

SHE: It's outrageous.

HE: Sorry?

SHE: I'm agreeing with you, I mean, it's ridiculous, outrageous.

HE: Oh ... yes ... we don't really know anything about the other person.

SHE: No, we don't.

HE: So, this pregnancy business ...

SHE: Don't call it that.

HE: Don't call it what?

SHE: "This pregnancy business." Don't call it that.

HE: Sorry.

SHE: *I can see the picture. The two us are lying on this bed and we're crying. Both of us. We're holding each other and crying. Because of the baby. Because it's so sad. We're saying things we would never ordinarily say. We're revealing amazing things from the depths of our beings. But he's sitting there with a pickle up his bum and I've got a pickle up my bum and there's a new kind of Berlin Wall between us. When do we get to the lovey-dovey part? And what about those great revelations?*

But ...

HE: But what?

SHE: But how do you feel?

HE: How do I feel?

SHE: Yes.

HE: Concerned.

SHE: Concerned?

HE: Yes, I'm very concerned about all this. Shouldn't I be?

SHE: I don't know if I want you to be concerned.

HE: What do you want me to be?

SHE: I don't know, I just ...

HE: You wanted to know what I thought.

SHE: Yes, it's just ...

HE: And I told you ...

SHE: I know, it's ...

HE: What?

SHE: I feel like this has happened for a reason, the timing is ... I can't tell you, it's like I've been wishing it without knowing it, like I asked for something and it happened.

HE: The cap didn't work.

SHE: But why now? I've been dreaming ... I wanted it somehow.

HE: Well, the next time you're moved to put the cap in sideways, I wish you'd let me know.

SHE: *Death is too good for him. Murder too gentle. I am a giant ice-pick. I am a study in scorn. I am covered with shards of broken glass, dirty flint designed to cause infected wounds that fester and cause limbs to be hacked off in muddy field hospitals with no anesthetic, not even a bullet to bite. He's screaming now as the saw cuts into his thigh.*

Excuse me, I have to go to the bathroom.

HE: *That was wrong. I can tell that was wrong. She didn't take it well, not well at all. It was supposed to be a joke. Maybe not a complete joke, some irony then to lighten the situation. I'm probably being insensitive. But she has to realize this is a pregnancy, not a New Age phenomena. All that thinking confuses her, but I can't be confused. There's not a confused bone in my body. I can see it's time for sensitivity. I've got to pour on the sensitivity.*

Maybe I'm not understanding you, explain it to me.

SHE: *The frost is so thick he'll never get through.*

It's not unknown, even in scientific circles, that thoughts can affect the body. It is possible to subconsciously desire something and have that thought result in a physical effect. But I assure you that I've never done anything to make this come about in a practical sense. I've always been very careful about birth control, always used protection, always made sure to check it.

HE: *She sounds like a nurse who's just killed the patient.*

SHE: I was on the pill for seven years, three doctors told me they wouldn't put an IUD in someone who hadn't had a child. AIDS or no AIDS, no man likes using a condom, they say they can't feel anything, you said that, so the cervical cap was a reasonable alternative.

Cervical dunce cap, there were times I'd check the bloody thing in the morning and it would be upside down.

HE: I'm sorry. I know you've been careful.

SHE: Tell me what you're feeling.

HE: Well, concerned.

SHE: *Never go out with a guy with a great record collection.*

HE: I'm trying to be plain. I think that's what's best now, even if it's hard. It's afterwards that I'm thinking about. There'll be morning sickness for a few months, then carrying the weight of it for another few months, then hours or days of screaming bloody agony and that's only the beginning. What about after?

SHE: You're younger than I am. It makes a difference.

HE: Aren't you tired?

SHE: No.

HE: I'm sorry I'm not more ... I want you to know that I'm there for ... anything you want. If you want to wake me up in the middle of the night ...

SHE: Let's just go to bed.

***

HE: *She doesn't want me to hold her but I can / hold her so beautifully ...*

SHE: *I don't want him to hold me / but he's holding me . . .*

HE: *I can feel it, drawing it out / of her ...*

SHE: *Making the nausea go / away, so beautiful ...*

HE: *I would feel it if I could, I'd rather I felt it than her / let me feel it ...*

SHE: *Like his / fingers had suction cups ...*

HE: *I can give her something, I can really / give something ...*

SHE: *He feels guilty and bad, / his arms are silk. Don't go away ...*

HE: *It's not fair she has to go through this, / it's not fair ...*

Time to get up?

SHE: Okay.

HE: I'm going to finish the rest of that piece today, get it over with this weekend.

SHE: *Death is too good for him.*

***

[Telephone conversation.]

HE: But I thought you wanted to be alone.

SHE: I want us to go through this together.

HE: You didn't want to be alone?

SHE: Maybe a bit, but then I didn't.

HE: You've got to tell me. All the women I've been with wanted to be alone all the time. I had to learn—"give them room."

SHE: I want this to mean something, be a way for us to talk, I want to know what you're feeling.

HE: I was trying to be plain.

SHE: I want to know all the contradictions, the feelings, I want to tell you mine. This will either break us apart, or make us closer than we ever would have been.

HE: Then you have to tell me things, like when you want to be alone and when you don't.

SHE: Okay, I will.

HE: I'm cancelling my plans for tonight. Let's go out to dinner and talk.

***

SHE: I didn't know there'd be so many mosquitoes. Look at that one. They love me, all that fresh flesh.

HE: Don't scratch. If you don't scratch right away they won't itch. That's a law of nature.

[HE sneezes.]

SHE: Oh, great, I bring you out here so we can talk and you turn into a city nerd.

HE: I love the country. Sorry about that restaurant, I just got claustrophobic. You want to know how I feel, it's hard to talk about how you feel, I don't know if I'm any good at it. Ouch! That one took a chunk out of me.

SHE: Do you want to go inside?

HE: No, it's fine. It's going to get dark soon.

SHE: Does it matter?

HE: No, I guess not. Sorry, I'm getting pedestrian.

SHE: I want to scratch so badly ...

HE: You have to use will-power.

SHE: I don't think I believe in will-power any more.

HE: About this whole business, I look at it all so differently than you, I don't believe in souls, or God. I hate it when people turn to religion as a way to get out of their own lives. I believe this is the life you have, no other, that you have to live it fully, deal with it, not turn to some big God up in the sky who's going to make it all better.

SHE: That's not what I think.

HE: I'm a pagan.

SHE: Pagans believe in something.

HE: You can't say "believe," you can say "have faith," but you can't say "believe."

SHE: *[Singing.]* You say tomato, I say tomato, tomato, tomato, potato, potato ...

HE: All right.

SHE: *[Still singing.]* Let's give the whole thing up.

HE: All right, I believe in this life.

SHE: This life?

HE: My life, our lives, not a bit of protoplasm that isn't conscious yet.

SHE: You can't be a pagan.

HE: All right, then I'm an atheist. Maybe I don't know what I am, that's one of the things I'd like to do this year, study up on this whole area.

SHE: But I'm pregnant now.

HE: All right, what's a pagan?

SHE: Okay, what I believe is …

HE: Not to interrupt you, but I'm getting eaten alive, let's walk over here.

SHE: Okay. They're playing baseball. It looks like something out of *Apocalypse Now*. In the middle of the jungle …

HE: The depo, the eerie light on the dancing girls …

SHE: I've always hated sports and games.

HE: Me too. Except chess.

SHE: Most of all I hate chess. But I believe in … okay, if I look up in the sky …

HE: Don't. That's what I hate, don't look up in the sky.

SHE: Alright. But I believe in … something.

HE: What?

SHE: Like a feeling.

HE: What kind of feeling?

SHE: A feeling of … things in the air.

HE: Like ghosts? Poltergeists? Pollen?

SHE: Don't.

HE: Sorry.

SHE: Like a feeling of … dreams and memory and … time and how it interrelates with … all that stuff about quantum physics … no, it's about that door, that door deep inside your stomach and it opens up and you feel nauseous and you feel other … realms … other frequencies playing on your life … like light and time and quantum physics ... you're a little girl in church, feeling things they weren't talking about, imagining beings everywhere and they protected you and guided you and you could talk to them and they could talk to you ... things, objects having power because they've been somewhere and retained or changed energy and you hold them in your hand and all of a sudden the top of your head is coming right off and you're thinking things you would never otherwise have thought ... and ... never doubting that "that feeling" would come if you called it. I'm not saying I've got it all figured out.

HE: Sorry, I turned off somewhere after quantum physics. It's like you're explaining the most dangerous kinds of superstition as if science supported ... as if it's some kind of way forward for mankind. It's like, you know when people say, "The last five times you called, I was thinking about you just before?" Well, what about the fifty times you called and they weren't thinking of you? It's a trap. I can see meditation, I learned meditation, but my mantra sounded like "shopping mall" and I started to laugh every time I said it.

SHE: So you abort your child and that's it.

HE: Don't do that. That's not what I said. Of course not, it's hard, and painful ...

SHE: But it has to be done, so bite the bullet old chap and ...

HE: I have my position.

SHE: I'm not talking about subscribing to the Pro Choice newsletter.

HE: I've dealt with these issues.

SHE: There's no question about the basic rights but I have a question about ...

HE: Many things start and never get finished. I don't want to go on about "freedom," I know it exists in different ways, but it's something they've written about through the ages and I've never had any. Always tried to be successful, tried to keep up, and now I'm stopping. I've dreamt of quitting that job for eons, and in four days, I'm finally going to do it. I want to work on my novel, travel, paint, take Japanese ... change my apartment ... I don't know ... be free. It's like I've been going down this long road, and I'm just smelling the sea, my head's exploding with plans and ideas and ...

SHE: I know. It's appalling timing.

HE: You could say that.

SHE: And you're younger than me.

HE: Not that much.

SHE: Younger. It counts. But you don't find that odd? That just when you have it all worked out in your head, some curve ball like this comes along?

HE: It's an accident. There's no plan out there that makes everything mean something.

SHE: I don't think I believe in accidents. I needed to know something. Either way I needed to know something.

HE: What?

SHE: It's not like that.

HE: Like what?

SHE: It's not a what, it's not a "like what" kind of thing.

HE: That's just fuzzy thinking.

SHE: Okay.

HE: You can't just say "Okay."

SHE: Yes I can. I can just say "Okay."

HE: And do I just sit back and wait for the verdict?

SHE: Let's keep it going.

HE: It's not a game.

SHE: We've got to keep it going, like a ball in the air, keep the balloon up until something changes. Until some purpose is clear. It's not really bad timing for me, it's terrible timing for you. Excuse me.

[SHE turns away, her hand on her mouth.]

HE: Are you all right?

SHE: Yes I'm fine.

HE: Did you eat something bad?

SHE: No.

HE: Are you getting the flu?

SHE: No.

HE: Oh.

SHE: Let's keep it going.

HE: Maybe we should stop.

SHE: I can't stop.

HE: Alright. Raising a child is about good timing for two people, a man and a woman. I never had a father. A child needs a mother and a father.

SHE: You get screwed up someway, I'm screwed up because I had a mother and a father ... ohhh look at that light, not like a sunset exactly. Magic time, that's what they call it in the movies. Oh, sorry, fuzzy thinking.

HE: Okay, you want to talk about learning things. Now I know I'd like to have kids someday, I didn't know that for sure before. But I think a child needs to be cared for. I know this may sound corny but I think of it like the

Darling family in *Peter Pan*, you know, the Walt Disney version? That Victorian house with the nursery?

SHE: The dog with the apron and Mr. and Mrs. Darling and they're going out and he can't fix his tie and he's pissed off ...

HE: The nursery is all set up for those kids, it's a place just for them, they're wanted and they know it.

SHE: And they fly out the window to become pirates and never go home.

HE: But they do go home.

SHE: Oh yeah, all except Peter Pan.

HE: I always thought I was Peter Pan.

SHE: I always thought I was. Maybe I just tell it to go away. Paula said she talked to it the night before, saying, "Next time, next time."

HE: That's the difference between us, I don't think there's an "it" to tell anything to.

SHE: All my friends who've had abortions say, "It would have been five." But like a question though, "It would have been eight?" It doesn't mean regret, not necessarily. If you've never had one, you feel kind of superior. You're all for the politics and all that, but deep down, you feel like you'd never actually do it ... until it happens and ...

HE: I understand fully the difficulty of the choice, as fully as I can, being a man. And I think, do I marry her and have people counting on their fingers?

SHE: People haven't counted on their fingers in twenty years.

HE: People will always be counting on their fingers.

SHE: What people? You mean your family?

HE: I don't just mean my family.

SHE: You're afraid to have your family know, in this day and age ...

HE: Aren't you afraid to have your family know?

SHE: If I really wanted this child, it would be easy, if I was sure. I could face down my family, friends, people. It would be in the greater cause, a noble thing, me, alone with my big belly facing the world. "Yes I want this child. No, the father doesn't want it, but I want it. I believe in life."

HE: It's like the invasion of the body snatchers, your zeal.

SHE: That's right, I've been invaded and boy, can I feel it.

HE: You know, I'm not completely oblivious, I feel protective of it too.

SHE: You what?

HE: I feel ...

SHE: You what?

HE: I feel vaguely protective of it too, but that doesn't mean I want to ...

SHE: You don't want to give me an inch, do you?

HE: I just don't think of it the way you do.

SHE: But how do you feel?

HE: Very concerned.

SHE: How can you listen to so much heavy metal and still sound like a banker?

HE: How do you feel?

SHE: ... happy.

HE: *Oh no, she's happy.*

***

SHE: Look at the moon.

Almost full, like me, almost full.

HE: Yeah.

She looks at the moon and thinks of the child, I look at the moon and think of escape.

***

HE: We just have to get up this hill.... Are you all right?

SHE: Yeah ... just a bit out of breath ... are we lost?

HE: Sorry ...

SHE: I love being lost.

HE: No, I'm just so sorry you have to go through all this, I can't imagine what you must be feeling. I ...

SHE: I'm not sorry.

HE: What do you mean?

SHE: I'm not "sorry" this happened.

HE: Well I guess I've betrayed myself then.

SHE: Let's go throw the I Ching.

HE: Okay.

***

HE: I've only done this once before.

SHE: It's all about creation.

HE: The Image is "Heaven above, heaven below." How do you know what it means?

SHE: *It means either way heaven. Either way. But I can't tell him that.*

HE: What does it mean?

SHE: I don't know.

***

SHE: He's pushing me into sounding positive that I want it. If he turned to me and said, "Don't kill my child, / let's get married, settle down and have babies for the rest of our lives ..."

HE: If I turned to her and said, "Okay, let's do it, we'll put the kid in a drawer, I'll marry you and we'll be joined in bliss for the rest of our lives ..." / She might just run like a rabbit.

SHE: I think I'd be running like a rabbit in the other direction.... / I know, I know, I'm thinking too much about what he wants, I'm not thinking about what I want ...

HE: No. She's not like that. She's operating on a higher plane. I'm the selfish one. She stands for life and I stand for pragmatism. / Disappointing. I'm disappointed in myself, hate that feeling.

SHE: But what he wants has to influence me about what I want. Doesn't it?

***

HE: It's like a nail being driven into my chest. Must have
exercised too hard. Shouldn't do the weights so fast,
got to build up slowly. OhhhhhhhhJesus that hurts. It's
not a heart attack. The last time it happened they said
my heart was fine. Acid in the stomach. Drinking too
much, it's quitting work, they're giving you the gears,
trying to make you weak, like them, weak. Hold to
your guns, don't let them tempt you, guilt you, stick to
your guns. What if she has it? Like Auschwitz I say,
live or die. There's no difference. All life is like
Auschwitz. They lined them up and said, "Live or die."
Can't be morbid, not the time to be morbid. My
stomach, it's in my stomach now. Let it go, let it go.
There's something wrong. I'll get it all done. I'll call
her, she wants me to check in, I'll check in. I'll listen.
I'm not a bastard, I'm not going to run. They're talking
about me, all those women friends of hers. About how
I don't want it. About what a bastard I am. How can you
be a man and not be a bastard? I am not a bastard. I am
not a bastard. In my stomach now, it's in my stomach.

***

SHE: Hi. How'd it go?

HE: They were fine, really. They gave me that inflatable
Paul McCartney over there. You could see they were
still a bit pissed off I was leaving, but they were fine,
really. So easy to end up forty with that hurt look in
your eyes.

SHE: No more day job. Hard to believe.

HE: It feels great. Do you want wine, beer, brandy ...

SHE: I'll just take bubbly water.

HE: I guess you're not drinking much.

SHE: No. Thanks for the roses. Reminded me of when we first met, except this time, the box was smaller?

HE: Short-stemmed. I have to be careful about money these days. We should get there early, there'll probably be a line-up.

SHE: Right.

HE: Enough of this lolling about.

SHE: I'm just learning to loll about.

HE: I guess I sound ...

SHE: Yeah.

HE: Private school does it to you, especially where I went, you try to rebel but if they get you at six years old, you're pretty well moulded. "Never explain, never complain." Remember when we first met, I said I wanted to learn to be more vulnerable?

SHE: Yes.

HE: I thought you could teach me, that you were vulnerable.

SHE: Did you?

HE: Yes.

SHE: It's just that you sounded like you had a list and vulnerable was on it.

HE: Look at this place. No life. It looks like I've had a day-job for fifteen years. It needs to be fixed up, new things, new looks, new life. The walls are boring, I should get the spray can out.

SHE: Why don't you?

HE: Great, she calls my bluff. All right, I will. That's all I need, for the landlord to come in, throw me out of here ... here we go. What should I do?

SHE: Whatever you want.

Talk to me, just talk to me.

HE: *You'd have my child, but you don't even like me.*

I want to write something that will remind me of the new life I'm starting, so I'll never go backwards. But it has to be done fully, the right colours, the right look, I don't want to be living with something ugly ... maybe I should just forget it.

SHE: *You really believe my having this child will ruin your life, don't you?*

HE: *Yes.*

SHE: What are you going to write?

HE: I'm not sure ...

SHE: What about "freedom"? I could do something.

HE: Why don't you?

SHE: No, it'd be too messy.

HE: Fuck it. Here goes ...

[HE sprays the wall.]

What do you think?

SHE: Zap?

HE: Maybe I'm not deep.

SHE: You're shaking.

HE: I get like that.

SHE: It's good. It really looks great.

HE: It could be better.

***

HE: *We can't talk about it all the time, we'd get too morose wandering around concentrating, going over it endlessly. We need a break from it all, a distraction.*

SHE: *But I'm pregnant, I'm pregnant, pregnant, there's no room for me if I'm pregnant pregnant pregnant.*

***

SHE: To bring the subconscious to the surface, Florite.
Amethysts for healing, feeling inside the body.
Carnelian for the sense of touch
into the fingers, into the skin.
Moonstones for the female parts,
deep inside, deep inside.
Celestite.
Azurite, Malachite dissolving secrets.
Crystal to see with,
crystal to see with,
crystal to clear the mind.

Into the darkness, into the dead baby dreams. Have to go there.

I'm twelve years old. The nuns have thin lips and sour faces. It's my fault, I'm being punished. Don't hurt the baby. I hate my belly, I hate the baby. She's got the voice of an angel. Don't look at me, don't look at me.

What are you saying? I remember you, hear you so I don't repeat? Repeat what? Now there's life down there ... have the child so that it's all new, washed free?

I don't want to feel death down there all my life, I want it to change. I want it to change. What if it's wrong? Ruin him, he thinks so, ruin me, ruin it. I can see his fear, smell it, it's real, I could hurt him. What if it's wrong to stop it? What if I never get over it, what if the dreams never go away, so that every time I see a baby I know ... I'm afraid to want it to be gone, then I'd be bad, they say I'm bad to want it to be gone, it feels awful to be bad. What if I have it only because I'm afraid to be bad? Everything will be better if I have a doll a baby, a baby doll. The baby will take everything, everything everything never have to think again if you have a baby doll. Never be alone again. It'll always want something, you always have to give something, it always has to take something, when you have a baby doll. It'll never go away for years and years, not for years, my baby doll.... Hello?

HE: Hi, it's me.

SHE: Hi.

HE: How are you doing?

SHE: It's been a bad day.

HE: I thought so when you didn't phone.

SHE: Yeah.

HE: Do you want to talk about it?

SHE: It's sort of hard on the telephone.

HE: You know I can't see you tonight, this dinner's been planned for weeks ...

SHE: It's okay.

HE: Don't do that. Tell me.

SHE: I just get caught down there, that's all.

HE: Down where?

SHE: In those dark places. I know I've never told you about the sessions with Peter. One time he took me into this ... past life or something.

HE: Uh huh.

SHE: I don't know if I'm making it up or not, he says it doesn't matter, but just before I ... conceived, I went back to this life again.

HE: What happened?

SHE: It's a kind of weird historical movie, too hard to explain.

HE: Tell me.

SHE: It's too hard to explain.

HE: I want to know.

SHE: I can't. Don't make me.

HE: I'm sorry, I won't probe in there if you don't want me to, I just thought it might help. If you let me in, you might be surprised with me.

SHE: I don't think so.

HE: Why?

SHE: You don't believe in magic.

***

HE: Our subconscious may be magical, that makes sense to me. I have a Tarot pack wrapped in yellow silk. I went out with a Hungarian countess who said she had the sight and used to want to make love on people's front lawns. I love Hallowe'en and Frankenstein. If it leads her down there, maybe it's wrong, maybe she shouldn't be down there. Maybe she likes being down there too much. It may not be such a dark tortured thing. After all, the origin of it is random. Life isn't sacred, when is it sacred in nature? I know what I want.

***

HE: Any new thoughts? I'm trying not to lean on you, trying not to load you down. I think, it's her decision, leave it to her. There's lots of things I think. Some of them pretty brutal.

SHE: Go ahead, be brutal, just know you can get brutality back.

HE: I wouldn't abandon you. You would have half of everything I earned.

SHE: Money isn't a question.

HE: I think it is.

SHE: That's not brutal.

HE: I think it is.

SHE: I keep trying to think of a way. I know what it makes sense to do, but I can't make it feel right. I've been wandering for a long time with no limitations, and it would be such a relief to say, "Sorry, I can't do it, I've got a kid."

HE: What kind of way?

SHE: Like we wouldn't have to live together, we could just go on the way we've been. You have your own place and work there, and stay over sometimes.

HE: I can just see myself, with you getting more and more visibly pregnant, coming over to visit and saying, "Hi, how're you doing?" And I think, do I leave town now, or help her through what could be a difficult pregnancy and then leave town? That's how bad it gets.

SHE: Sometimes I wish you were a one-night stand and didn't have any feelings and would just go away.

HE: That's what really bothers me. The way you talk about it, as if it has no rights. I can't go along with your seat-of-the-pants ideas about raising a child. The more I think about it the more I know I'd want money for a child, and a good place to live, and planning and ideas about schools and ...

SHE: What seat-of-the-pants ideas?

HE: Ad hoc child-raising. Some romantic idea of solving your life with a child.

SHE: I turned down a twenty-thousand-dollar job last month, a choice I would reverse if I had a reason to do things just for money. I have a strong community of friends that I value. The child wouldn't be without some very strong male models. I think I have morals of a kind, maybe wouldn't be a very traditional mother, but I think I have something to offer a child. I may act like I don't really have a hold on things. But I've got money in my RSP account, and I do keep it together in the regular world.

HE: Yes you do. And I'm nowhere near that. I'm just beginning. Maybe in a few years, if everything works out with us, there's a possibility for children then.

SHE: But there's no guarantee of that.

HE: No. Are you all right?

SHE: Yeah, it's just that chemotherapy feeling.

HE: Is there anything I can do?

SHE: Just go to sleep.

***

HE: When I look in the mirror, I see a boy's face. In a couple of years, it'll be a man's.

SHE: Why not now?

***

SHE: I just have to get through the archway... I'm on my hands and knees kind of pushing back and forth ... they stick their hands up ... I heave and hea—

HE: Wake up.

SHE: What?

HE: You were talking in your sleep.

SHE: What did I say?

HE: I don't know, I couldn't make out a word.

***

HE: My mother is my best friend.

SHE: Then why can't you tell her?

***

SHE: Hello?

HE: Hi, it's me.

SHE: Hi.

HE: Has it been a hard day?

SHE: Sort of.

HE: Would you like to go to a movie tomorrow night?

SHE: I'll have to see how I feel.

HE: Are you feeling all right?

SHE: I can never tell when it's going to hit me.

HE: You know you can call me any time, / wake me up, even in the middle of the night.

SHE: I know. Thanks. / Well, I better let you go.

HE: I'll see you tomorrow.

SHE: Bye.

HE: Bye.

***

SHE: *Hello?*

HE: *Hi, it's me.*

SHE: *Hi.*

HE: *How are you?*

SHE: *Pregnant. How are you?*

HE: *Constipated, pains in my stomach, in my chest.*

SHE: *Sick as a dog, I nearly passed out in the bank today.*

HE: *I can't stand it when you tell me things like that.*

SHE: *Don't worry, I'll probably "arrest the foetus." I'm just dragging it out for the fun of it, and to watch you squirm.*

HE: *You don't know how good I'm being to you, I call every day.*

SHE: *You don't know how good I'm being to you, I could fuck you good.*

HE: *All this trouble from one fuck.*

SHE: *Hard to fucking believe.*

***

SHE: Jim would have it.

HE: Who's Jim?

SHE: I could just go up to him and say, "Listen, I'm pregnant and I need a father. Let's live together and give it a go." That's the way I feel right now. Fuck it. Do you really think you'll find the right person after years of careful planning and it'll all work out to your advantage? I could have a good life with him. Very Victorian isn't it? "We didn't exactly 'love' each other at first, but time passed and something changed ..." A good life. With a good man.

HE: *Now I know how they get strangled.*

You don't think he'd be put off by a potential mother with five therapists who has to hang signs saying "breathe" around her apartment in case she forgets?

SHE: No.

HE: Someone who needs eleven hours' sleep and takes two hours to get out of bed in the morning?

SHE: I can get out of bed if I want to.

HE: Someone who can't go to sleep at night without the light on, who eats Valium like candy, with inexplicable pains, insomnia, flus that don't go away for months ...

SHE: People change.

HE: Those things wouldn't happen when you carry this child?

SHE: No.

HE: They wouldn't affect you and the child afterward when you're post-natally depressed and exhausted? And there's not enough money to get a babysitter and it's no longer groovy to have a child, and you can't work at home and there's no one to help …

SHE: And I haven't slept in days and I'm sitting on the floor crying with the baby in my arms crying and the place smells like shit and urine and the floor is crusty with spit and apple juice and crackers and I've already called all my friends for a thousand emergencies and the last guy just left because he wanted someone with no attachments and the kid is ugly and looks like neither of us and they think there's something wrong with him, and there's no one no one no one, and I'm banging my head against the wall then I take the kid to do the same thing …

HE: Stop it. There's nothing down there but dirt and hate and craziness.

SHE: Don't try to out-imagine me in the dark places. There's nowhere you can go that I haven't been.

HE: You've never even looked at me. I can't bear to have my own child born. How dark is that?

***

SHE: Tell someone.

HE: I can't.

SHE: A friend, an enemy, a total stranger.

HE: I can't. I'm not that kind of person.

***

HE: Are you talking to that therapist about this?

SHE: I can't help it. But I'm very wary. If he shows signs of moral judgement, I get pissed off and back away.

HE: So am I in competition with him?

SHE: I don't think we should think in terms of competition.

HE: Sorry, I just ... what do I do? Wait for the verdict?

SHE: We talk about it. We talk about it until we can't talk any more.

***

SHE: *Tell me what you feel ...*

HE: *This is where they get you.*

SHE: *That's all I want to know, what you feel / tell me your doubts ...*

HE: *When they want to suck you dry of all your secrets.*

SHE: *Let me know that you have doubts, then it / will be better ...*

HE: *She's dying for it, dying to have me tell her about my childhood ...*

SHE: *It's too awful thinking you / have no doubts ...*

HE: *She wants the hurt places, she wants the scrapes the scars the wounds the memories that bite and claw, she wants the dirt. Then she'll probe in there for a reason why she should have it.*

SHE: *I could walk to that abortion singing, if you let it in. Say it's with / regret you see me go.*

HE: *Maybe there's no underlying anything to me. Maybe I'm a dry well of self-conscious tragedy. I just don't want a child right now!*

SHE: What are you thinking?

HE: I'm thinking that I have no control.

SHE: Are you kidding? I'm not really a free spirit, you know, I'm much more of a traditional woman than you think. You've got much too much control.

***

SHE: *I don't know why I fucked anyone. I don't know why I fucked him. You hold them off for four weeks and they're moaning, "How can you be so cruel? Why can't you let me in?" Four weeks, if you're lucky, to decide. Then the night comes and you both know and somebody lights a candle. And there's a great couple of days when you lie around in bed and touch and talk, and go to the bathroom with the door open. I love that part. And I pay for it. Because then they become "them." I'm twelve years old, I don't want anyone to put that inside me. I only want a father, to play with and to hold me, to tell stories, to have fun. I only want a father, not a lover, not a boyfriend, not a baby. A father, a playmate, a love.*

HE: *I know what I want. I can't do what I want. Run run run / run to the farthest corner of the globe fly away and come back in twenty years.*

SHE: *Get on a plane a boat, a train a bus, never tell anyone where you are, run away with your secret that soon won't be a secret when will this adolescence end I don't want to fly out the nursery window, yes I do I still do, no big belly / just me I'm flying so far so high ...*

HE: *I hate the thought of touching, don't want to touch anything, don't like the smell of food who am I that I can't come through what kind of selfish prig am I that I can't come through, tell me what you're thinking, I'm here for you tell me what you're thinking I'll phone you every day tell me what you're thinking / tell me what you're feeling tell me what you're thinking tell me what you're feeling tell me what you're thinking tell me what you're feeling, tell me what you're thinking ...*

SHE: *I can't climb out the window's stuck the nursery is empty the baby is dead I can't tell you you'd be afraid you're too young, my baby, you're too young. What am I feeling? I'm pregnant pregnant pregnant pregnant pregnant pregnant pregnant pregnant pregnant pregnant pregnant pregnant.*

HE: How are you today?

SHE: Fine. Okay, a little weird.

HE: How do you mean, weird?

SHE: It's been a hard, day, that's all.

***

HE: It's ridiculous, I can't get away from it.

SHE: I know. I've never seen so many pregnant women waddling around. Or babies.

HE: Everywhere I look. Did you see the cover of the

National Enquirer this week?

SHE: "Two-headed woman becomes pregnant. One head wants it, the other doesn't."

HE: It's a good thing we still have our sense of humour.

***

SHE: I don't know who I'm speaking to, goddess, god, spirits, trees, all the books I've read. God. God of my childhood. For the first time, I asked you to heal me, and then I got pregnant. It seems that having this child would heal me, but I think that's not quite right. I know this is a gift. A gift. Don't let me twist it around. Heaven above, heaven below. I feel you, all the space around me, within me, the universe we know and the universe beyond, all the energy of all there is. Do I have your gift sucked out of me or is it your gift that it's sucked out so I will finally be empty? Is it your gift for me to know this death? Or is this moment your gift? Heaven above, heaven below. Accept the gift. That's all I know.

***

HE: Semen semen semen, spread all over the ground. Semen alone, semen in eggs, lost semen, lost cocks of lost fathers of lost children without fathers. Boys at school laughing, but who is your father? What is your name? Everyone knows the name comes from the father like the semen comes from the father, like heaven is ruled over by the Father. Dad? You out there? I'm going to start it all again. I need a father. Dad? I want to talk to you, Dad. Let's have a father-son talk. Are you there? Where were you to say, "This child is mine"? This boy is mine. I am a male and this is my male child. No, you couldn't claim me, you couldn't claim that horror. I repeat the cycle, the circle, if she has it. To you my child, I hand down my hole in the guts. A legacy. I know exactly how it will feel, I know exactly how you will feel. Very specific feeling really. I hand you down my pain in the guts. And you will live as I have lived, and one day you will turn and run. Because you were handed down a hole, a pain, a lost cock never there, never waiting, never wanting. The cock that wanted to fuck but not to breed. And if I stay, you'll know, and if I leave, you'll know. And I'll know, and she'll know. Don't do it. Don't do it. Don't do it.

***

SHE: There's no such thing as rock and roll.

HE: What?

SHE: There's no such thing as rock and roll. There's no such thing as The Beatles.

HE: I wouldn't go that far.

SHE: Of course not.

HE: Well, they were legitimized by their generation, the important thing to remember is where it all came from, black music, R and B. Now, The Rolling Stones were ...

SHE: Oh, I don't care.

HE: That's the thing, your generation ...

SHE: My generation?

HE: Tail end of the sixties.

SHE: Oh, for Christ's sake, pretty tail if you ask me.

HE: You smoke marijuana, like to lie around and pretend there's nothing to do, hate ambition.

SHE: I don't hate ambition. I hate your kind of ambition.

HE: Punks like speed ...

SHE: I've done every conceivable kind of ...

HE: All that phoney gentleness, punk is angry.

SHE: Punk is dead.

HE: I was one of the first to say punk is dead, but it exposed all that wishy washy hippie bullshit, brought it back to anger. Kids understand that today, they're angry.

SHE: I finally figured out your routine, I saw this phrase in a trendy magazine, and I understood. "Fusion Punk."

HE: That's already outdated.

SHE: Not on enough for the nineties?

HE: Well, I finally understood your little routine, you've already made the appointment, haven't you?

SHE: Yes ... but that doesn't mean ...

HE: Then what the fuck have you been putting us through this for?

SHE: I thought I should make it right away so we could cancel if we decided ... like a failsafe ...

HE: You lied, you've been lying all along.

SHE: So I wouldn't be walking around for a month with it growing larger and then make the appointment and then wait and ...

HE: "I want us to go through this together, it'll make us closer." But you've got something up your sleeve ...

SHE: I wanted to go through every thought, I wanted—

HE: What?

SHE: Contact.

HE: You made your decision the minute you heard, didn't you?

SHE: It wasn't like that. Yes, I thought I should make the appointment right away but I really thought that we might be cancelling that appointment, I didn't know, I still don't know ...

HE: Say it, just say it.

SHE: Yes I knew. Not the first minute, but the minute after. You're right. I'm a liar, somewhere I am a liar.

HE: Stop being so noble, get angry. Hate me.

SHE: I don't hate you.

HE: I think you do, right now, I think you do.

SHE: No.

HE: Say it.

SHE: Okay, I hate you.

HE: I can't get hold of you, there's something ...

SHE: What?

HE: Two-faced.

SHE: I hate you. I hate you. You're such a pompous fake. I hate you. I hate men. Say it, say what we're going to do. It's a four-letter word. Say it.

HE: I don't know what you ...

SHE: Yes you do. Say it.

HE: Kill.

SHE: Killing is a part of things. Of everything there is?

HE: Yes.

SHE: Do you believe that's true?

HE: Yes. Do you?

SHE: Yes.

HE: I think you've been very brave.

SHE: Fuck off.

HE: What's that?

SHE: It's the instructions the doctor gave me. All the things you're supposed to do.

HE: Are you doing it because I bullied you into it?

SHE: No. I just can't believe you're not sorry.

Is he / going to give in? Give in …

HE: *Don't dare move …*

SHE: *Give in, say you / regret it …*

HE: *I don't regret / it …*

SHE: *Say "it," say there's an it. / Say you're sorry, say you're sorry …*

HE: *There's no "it." / I'm sorry for you. Sorry for …*

SHE: *You think I would grab onto one tiny word?*

HE: *Yes.*

SHE: *You're right.*

HE: *Do you want this child?*

SHE: *No.*

Look at the rainbows. The prism makes them such a funny shape, kind of fat.

HE: They're like little beings from outer space.

HE: They're trying to communicate with us.

SHE: Beep, beep beep beep ...

HE: Beep beep, take us to your leader... beep beep beep.

SHE: Beep beep beep.

[They hold each other.]

Last night I dreamt of a little boy, toddler sized, all bundled up in a red snow suit. I only saw his back, he was just walking away. I think I made that appointment a long long time ago. When you became the father, I started to see you, I think I see you now.

HE: Once I asked my mother's friend, "Do you know where my father is?" I was four years old. And they found him and made him visit me. I was insane with joy. But he couldn't look at me. He sat around with the friends who had brought him and played cards. I kept running into the kitchen to look at him. He'd turn around and go, "Hi there." He tried to talk to me but he couldn't. Couldn't look and couldn't talk. Just an introverted kind of person with his own problems, how could he relate to me? I went into the bedroom and bent over by the bed, laid my head down on the covers. I stayed there till they found me and made me throw darts at a board. Somewhere in all that time, he left. Rock and roll helped. Music helped. I was the guy drinking beer with the bands backstage because I likened their lyrics to Proust. My head is full of trivia about who played bass with The Cramps and why Johnny Rotton learned to play piano. But how long is a generation in that world? Two years. Because in two years you neither know nor truly care what bands are starting out anymore. It helped, but it's a trap if you're not in the band. You're either in the band or out of the band.

SHE: I thought you were a candidate.

HE: Please don't be offended if I ask you to blow your nose.

***

HE: We should get to a seven-thirty show so we can get to bed at a reasonable hour. I think that's best.

SHE: Okay.

HE: What do you want to see?

SHE: Nothing too …

HE: No.

SHE: Something …

HE: Yeah … nothing too …

SHE: There must be something good on like that.

HE: There must be. There's, *Your Turn Now* at seven-fifteen.

SHE: What's that about?

HE: It's a British film about a father who beats his children.

SHE: No …

HE: Well, there's *Cock and Bull Story*, you wanted to see that.

SHE: Yeah, I know, I just don't know if it's too …

HE: It's not really that violent, all the violence is at the beginning.

SHE: But you've already seen it.

HE: I don't mind. He's gay and his lover kills him but it's really about their relationship.

SHE: Can't I just wait to decide? There're five movies we could see, they're all at the same place ...

HE: They're all at different times, though, we'd end up waiting around and I don't think you're up to that.

SHE: No. Actually, I did want to see *Cock and Bull Story* and if it's a good movie, it's a good movie, right? I mean, it will feel good to see something good as opposed to something light that's not good. That never really makes you feel good.

HE: Then it's decided?

***

HE: *Somewhere someone is running into the other room, it's someone like me but it isn't me. He's saying, "No, stop, we'll have it, we'll work it out. It's all right." I hold my ear to her stomach the way everyone is doing, the way everyone is doing out there in the world, we do it too. But it's not me. I can be strong tomorrow. That's all. Let it be easy, let there be no pain, let it be over. Whatever it is she believes in, let it protect us both.*

SHE: *Speak softly,*
   to the little one,
   sea anemone,
   don't be afraid to picture it,
   think of it,
   eight weeks' worth.

Say,
I ask you to leave,
flow out of me like rain like water like mucus like blood.
This is such a short time for you.
Become a memory for me.
And a goal a goad, that life may be good,
unshared by you.
I am saying,
"No child now."
This good girl will never be totally good again,
I will know the dark
eye of the Mother,
carrying the balance of so much,
but always so, always so, always so.
I am an earthquake,
I am a tidal wave,
I am hail, and frost,
I am the twisting volcano.
I give up the act, I give it up, I give it up,
I give you up, I give you up.
Creator take you, sky enfold you, stars remember you.
Tomorrow we will die.
Go gentle into that good night.

***

HE: I have tomorrow and the next day totally free.

***

SHE: I forgot to take off my underpants, they're putting
them in a brown paper bag with my name written on it.
I wonder if they'll remember to give them to me? It

doesn't matter, I brought clean ones in my purse. My mother's daughter.

HE: I forgot to buy mineral water. She'll come home and be thirsty and want mineral water. I've got everything else. Good things. Healthy things. Cheese and bread and fruit and yoghurt.

SHE: The anesthetist is looking at me carefully, telling me what he's going to do. The nurse with the blonde ponytail is so different. Human and kind without being sucky. I just love her. She has the voice of an angel.

HE: I don't know anything. I didn't ask her anything. Is this the kind with the needle? Do they still do it that way? Do they put the needle right up? Will she be awake? Is she going to see it? How much will it hurt? Oh, let them do it to me. I'd rather they did it to me.

SHE: She puts a needle in my hand, it's longer than the other ones, and they leave it in. / The lights should be different. Too bright.

HE: It's now, it's happening now.

SHE: How will it be / when I wake up?

HE: What if something goes wrong?

SHE: Sometimes people dry heave for hours / from the anesthetic ...

HE: Sometimes they're fine almost immediately. Sometimes they're fine.

SHE: She tells me gently, "We're adding the anesthetic to the IV now." It's mixed in with the liquid, moonstone white in its plastic bag.

HE: Tired, so tired I can't be tired, it must be the exercise, the shopping the not sleeping last night ...

SHE: I can feel it coming, the room is whirling ...

HE: The person says, "The last five times I thought of you, you called just after." What about the fifty times that ...

SHE: I'm fighting it for a bit, so inevitable.

> *[SHE lights the sage, the smoke rises.]*

Up, up so high, so far ...

HE: Gentle ...

> *[SHE smudges herself, HE smudges himself, SHE waves the smoke toward the audience.]*

SHE: Tell me that you love me.

HE: I love you.

SHE: I love you.

> *[SHE blots the sage.]*

Are we grown up now?

> *[Blackout.]*

MORE CANADIAN DRAMA TITLES
available from Blizzard Publishing

Gravel Run
Conni Massing
$10.95 (pb) 921368–16–X

Amigo's Blue Guitar
Joan McLeod
$9.95 (pb) 929091–34–5

The Invention of Poetry
Paul Quarrington
$9.95 (pb) 929091–31–0

Memories of You
Wendy Lill
$9.95 (pb) 929091–06–X

Fire
Paul Ledoux and
David Young
$9.95 (pb) 929091–05–1

Midnight Madness
Dave Carley
$9.95 (pb) 920197–88–4

Departures and Arrivals
Carol Shields
$10.95 (pb) 921368–13–5

The Soft Eclipse
Connie Gault
$9.95 (pb) 921368–14–3

Prairie Report
Frank Moher
$10.95 (pb) 921368–15–1

Beautiful Lake Winnipeg
Maureen Hunter
$9.95 (pb) 921368–10–0

*Unidentified Human
Remains and the True
Nature of Love*
Brad Fraser
$10.95 (pb) 921368–11–9

Exile
Archie Crail
$9.95 (pb) 921368–12–7

Bordertown Café
Kelly Rebar
$10.95 (pb) 921368–08–9

The Mail Order Bride
Robert Clinton
$10.95 (pb) 921368–09–7

Sky
Connie Gault
$10.95 (pb) 921368–06–2

*The Chinese Man Said
Goodbye*
Bruce McManus
$8.95 (pb) 921368–05–4

Footprints On the Moon
Maureen Hunter
$9.95 (pb) 921368–07–0

The Third Ascent
Frank Moher
$9.95 (pb) 921368–04–6

refugees
Harry Rintoul
$7.95 (pb) 921368–02–X